THE BIG BOOK OF

DINOSAURS

A First Book for Young Children

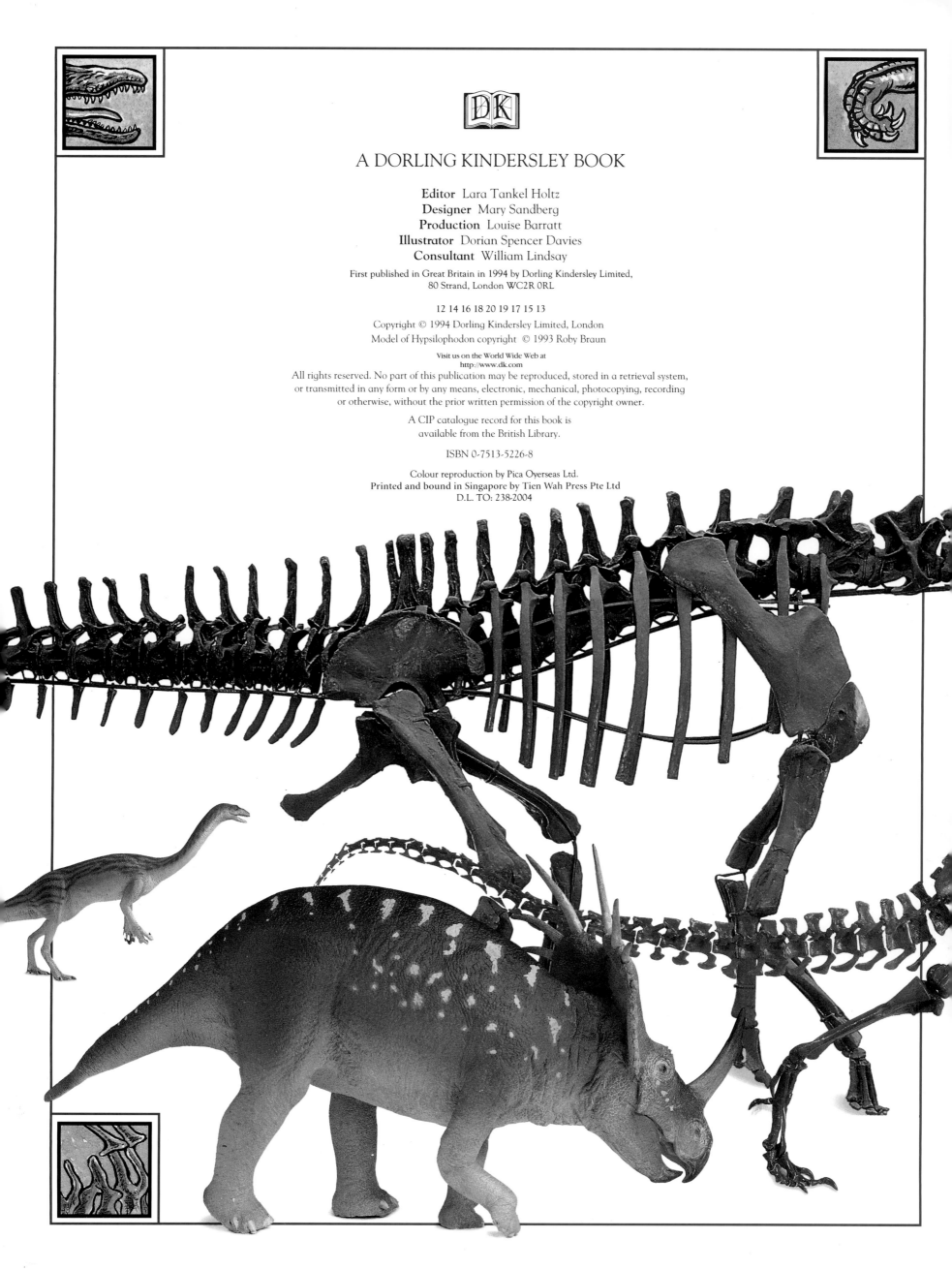

DK

A DORLING KINDERSLEY BOOK

Editor Lara Tankel Holtz
Designer Mary Sandberg
Production Louise Barratt
Illustrator Dorian Spencer Davies
Consultant William Lindsay

First published in Great Britain in 1994 by Dorling Kindersley Limited,
80 Strand, London WC2R 0RL

12 14 16 18 20 19 17 15 13

ISBN 0-7513-5226-8

Colour reproduction by Pica Oyerseas Ltd.
Printed and bound in Singapore by Tien Wah Press Pte Ltd
D.L. TO: 238-2004

THE BIG BOOK OF
DINOSAURS

A First Book for Young Children

Angela Wilkes

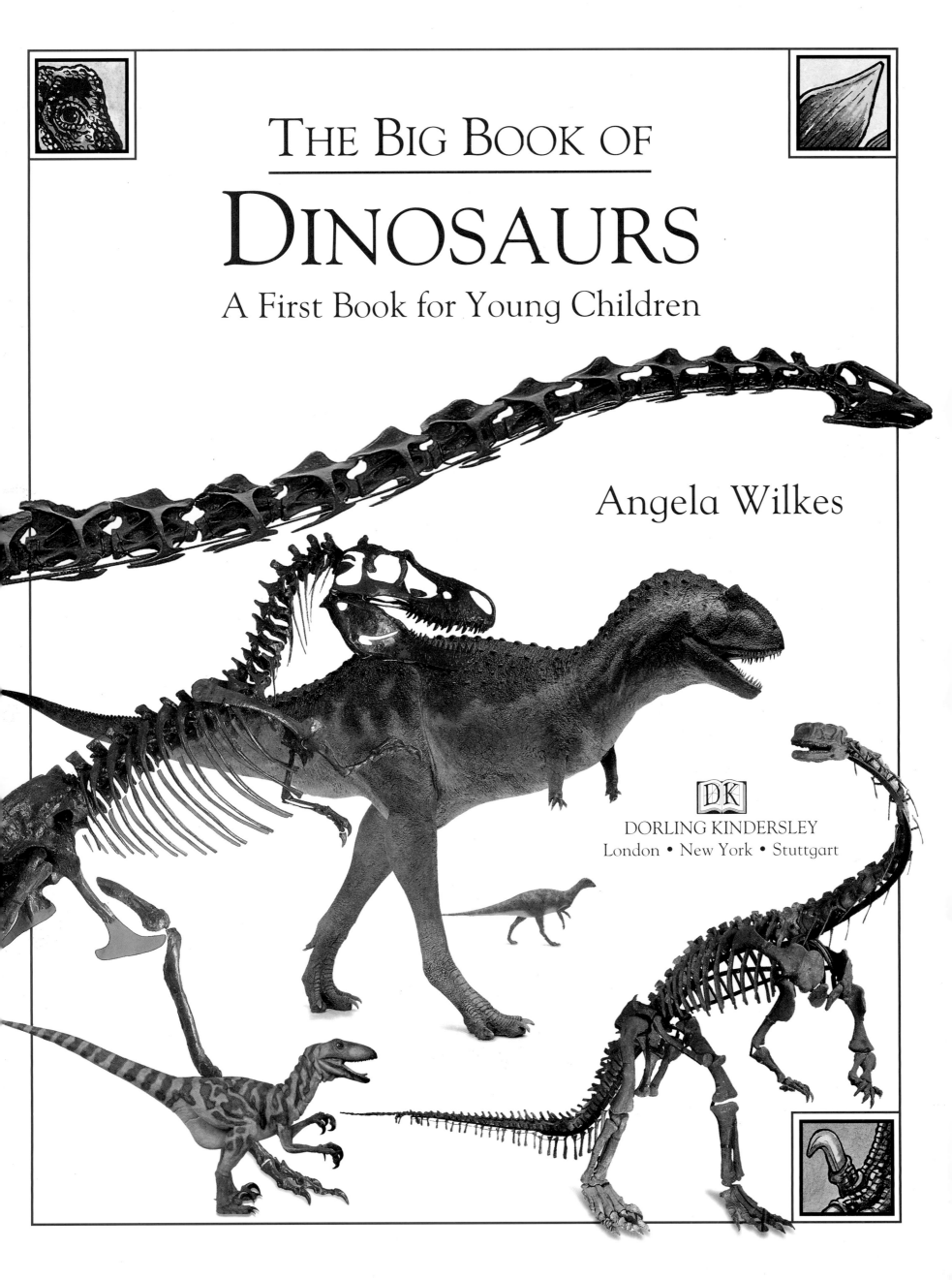

DK
DORLING KINDERSLEY
London • New York • Stuttgart

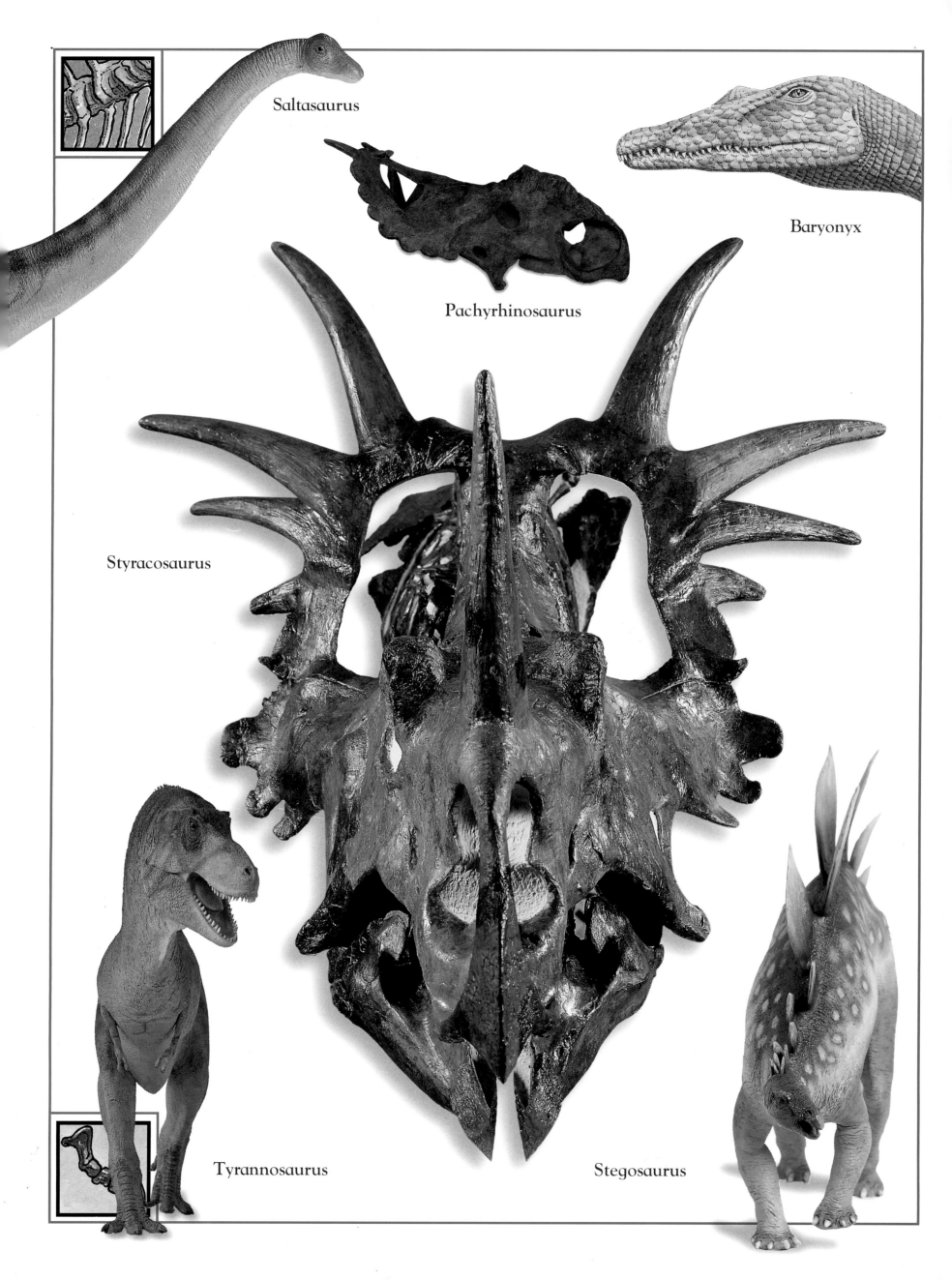

Saltasaurus

Baryonyx

Pachyrhinosaurus

Styracosaurus

Tyrannosaurus

Stegosaurus

Gallimimus

Coelophysis

Iguanodon

Contents

Psittacosaurus

Compsognathus

Baryonyx claw

Megalosaurus tooth

Prenocephale

Oviraptor

Stegoceras

Apatosaurus thumb

Leaellynasaura

Dinosaur clues

This hole shows where the dinosaur's eye was.

Clues to the past

How do we know so much about dinosaurs when the last ones died millions and millions of years ago? Scientists hunt for the fossil remains of dinosaur bones and teeth, buried in rocks. They use these clues to find out as much as they can about dinosaurs.

Tyrannosaurus' huge jaw and sharp teeth show that it was a fierce meat-eater.

Tyrannosaurus skull

Rebuilding a dinosaur

Scientists can fit together a dinosaur's fossil bones to build a life-size skeleton. They can make models of any bones that are missing.

heavy tail, to help balance the body

tail bones

foot bone

heavy claws

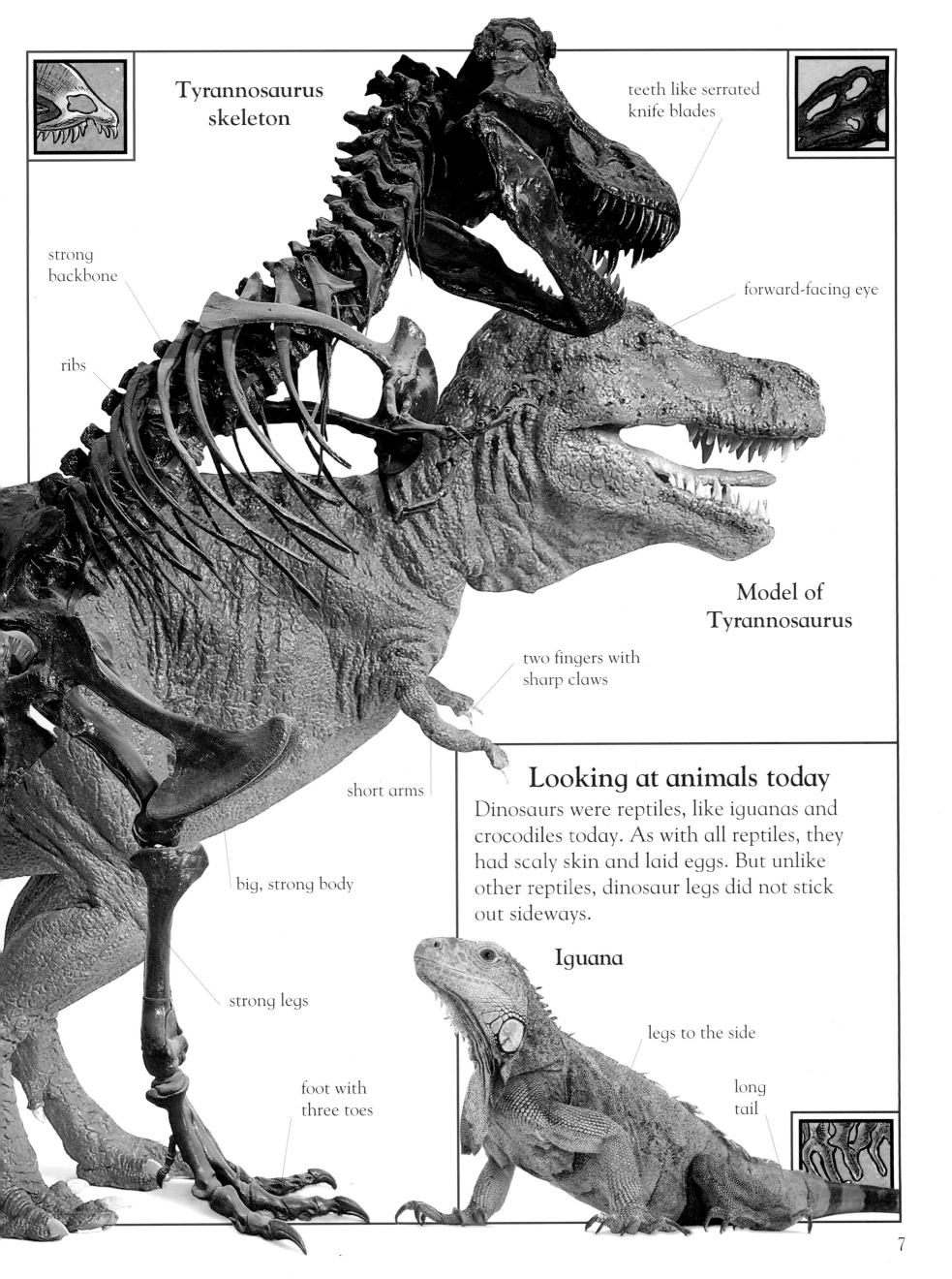

Tyrannosaurus
skeleton

teeth like serrated
knife blades

strong
backbone

ribs

forward-facing eye

Model of
Tyrannosaurus

two fingers with
sharp claws

short arms

Looking at animals today

Dinosaurs were reptiles, like iguanas and crocodiles today. As with all reptiles, they had scaly skin and laid eggs. But unlike other reptiles, dinosaur legs did not stick out sideways.

big, strong body

Iguana

strong legs

legs to the side

long
tail

foot with
three toes

Face to face

Portrait gallery

The dinosaurs shown on this page were all different shapes and sizes. Some had spikes to defend themselves, others had bony lumps for protection, some had many sharp teeth, while others had no teeth at all.

Euoplocephalus

Euoplocephalus was an armoured dinosaur covered in bony lumps and bumps.

Triceratops

This big plant-eater had a head frill and three sharp horns.

Corythosaurus

This duckbilled dinosaur had a head crest like a plate standing on edge.

Stegosaurus

This plant-eater had two rows of plates down its back.

Oviraptor

Oviraptor was a two-legged hunter with a strange beak and a crest on its head.

toothless beak

Compsognathus

Fierce and tiny Compsognathus was no bigger than a hen.

Gallimimus

This dinosaur, with its beaky face and long neck, looked like an ostrich.

Lesothosaurus

This small dinosaur was an agile runner.

Edmontonia

Edmontonia had a tough armour of bony plates and fierce spikes.

Iguanodon

Iguanodon was a big, plant-eating dinosaur with many strong teeth and spiked thumbs.

Pachycephalosaurus

This dinosaur had a strange, bony head that looked like a crash helmet.

Barosaurus

This gigantic plant-eater had a neck more than nine metres long.

Fast and fierce

Deinonychus

Deinonychus was a fast and very fierce dinosaur. It attacked its prey by slashing out with the long, curved claws on its feet. It had razor-sharp teeth for tearing off chunks of flesh.

Troodon's large eyes faced forwards.

Troodon

This quick-witted dinosaur had a very big brain. Its large eyes helped it to hunt for prey at night.

Deinonychus had 70 jagged teeth for eating tough prey.

These fearsome claws were as long as your whole hand.

Dromaeosaurus

This skull shows that Dromaeosaurus had powerful jaws lined with saw-edged teeth.

Deinonychus used this sharp claw to slash its victims.

Ornitholestes

Ornitholestes was light and speedy with a very long tail. It probably hunted small reptiles.

Herrerasaurus used its long tail to help it balance.

Herrerasaurus

Herrerasaurus was one of the first dinosaurs, living 225 million years ago. It was as big as a small car and had sharp teeth and claws.

What do you think Herrerasaurus used its strong, curved claws for?

Compsognathus had a narrow head.

Compsognathus

Compsognathus lived 150 million years ago and was no bigger than a hen. It could run very swiftly to catch small lizards and insects to eat.

Long legs and feet helped Compsognathus to run quickly.

Beaky dinosaurs

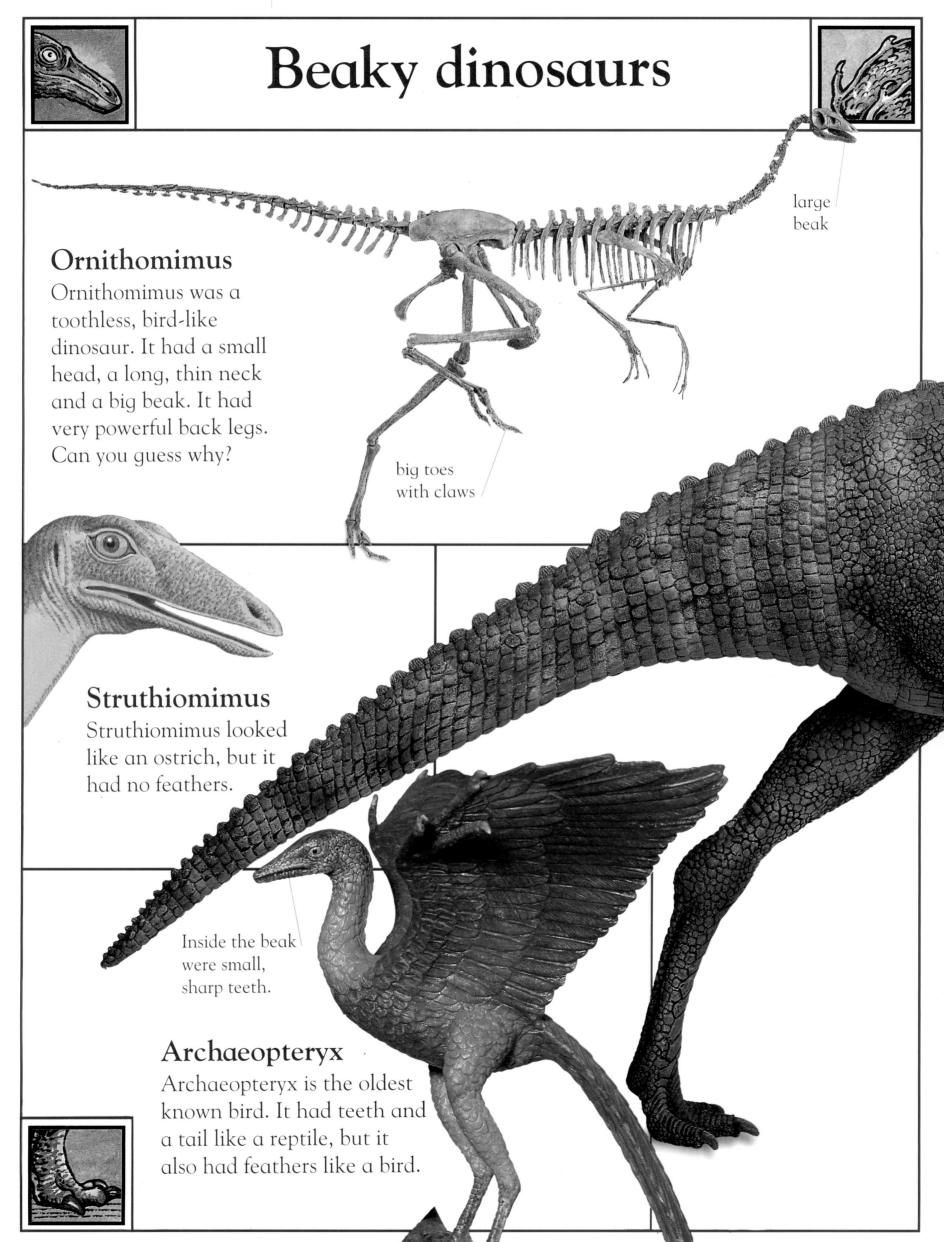

large beak

Ornithomimus

Ornithomimus was a toothless, bird-like dinosaur. It had a small head, a long, thin neck and a big beak. It had very powerful back legs. Can you guess why?

big toes with claws

Struthiomimus

Struthiomimus looked like an ostrich, but it had no feathers.

Inside the beak were small, sharp teeth.

Archaeopteryx

Archaeopteryx is the oldest known bird. It had teeth and a tail like a reptile, but it also had feathers like a bird.

Gallimimus

Gallimimus looked like a very big ostrich. It was a fast runner and could have kept up with a race-horse. Gallimimus probably ate insects and lizards as well as some plants.

small head and long, toothless beak

Oviraptor

Oviraptor is known as the "egg thief". It may have stolen and eaten the eggs of horned dinosaurs.

Oviraptor's bony crest was perched on its nose.

strong, curved claws

Dromiceiomimus

Dromiceiomimus was another "ostrich" dinosaur. But unlike ostriches, all these dinosaurs had arms and hands with claws.

long neck, like an ostrich

toothless, beaky skull

Terrible teeth

Tyrannosaurus

Scientists can tell what kind of food an animal eats by looking at its teeth. Tyrannosaurus had huge jaws that could open very wide and long, saw-edged teeth. What do you think it ate?

Tyrannosaurus' eyes faced forwards. This helped it to judge distances when attacking its prey.

These jaws were strong enough to crush bones.

Megalosaurus

Megalosaurus' teeth were curved like daggers. When a tooth broke or wore out a new one grew in its place.

fossilized Megalosaurus tooth

Tyrannosaurus' teeth were as long as table knives.

Allosaurus

Allosaurus was a savage meat-eater. Its teeth were sharp and saw-edged for slicing through flesh. They curved backwards to give Allosaurus a firm grip on its victims.

serrated, blade-like teeth

Diplodocus

Diplodocus was an enormous plant-eater. It had thin teeth, like small pencils, for raking up leaves and ferns.

Diplodocus only had teeth at the front of its mouth.

toothless beak

Compsognathus

This little meat-eater had small, sharp teeth. It probably ate big insects and lizards.

pointed fangs

cheek teeth for grinding

Heterodontosaurus

Heterodontosaurus was an unusual plant-eater. It had a horny beak, and three kinds of teeth for cutting and grinding.

Mighty meat-eaters

Carnotaurus' head looked like a bull's head.

Carnotaurus

The fiercest dinosaurs were the two-legged meat-eaters such as this Carnotaurus. It had a big head, strong legs, and short arms. It hunted other dinosaurs or ate dead animals that it found.

Dilophosaurus

Dilophosaurus means "two-ridge lizard". It gets its name from the two crests on its head, rather like two plates standing on edge.

Allosaurus

Allosaurus lived in North America 150 million years ago. It attacked and ate big plant-eaters like Diplodocus.

Ceratosaurus

Ceratosaurus had a short, thick neck, a huge head, and a bony horn on its snout.

Dilophosaurus used its long teeth and sharp claws to attack its prey.

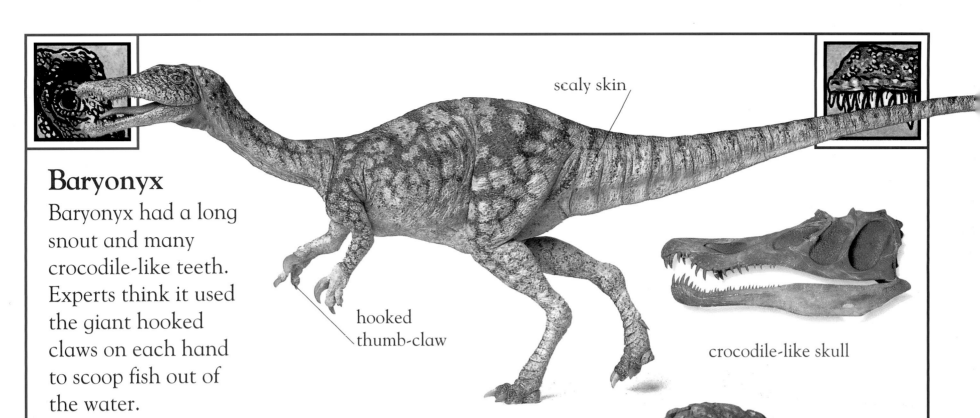

Baryonyx

Baryonyx had a long snout and many crocodile-like teeth. Experts think it used the giant hooked claws on each hand to scoop fish out of the water.

scaly skin

hooked thumb-claw

crocodile-like skull

Tyrannosaurus' massive jaws bared rows of fangs as it moved in to attack its victims.

Tyrannosaurus

Tyrannosaurus was the biggest and strongest meat-eating animal ever – nearly as tall as a double-storey house. Although it was very heavy, scientists think it could sprint over short distances to catch slow-moving dinosaurs.

Biggest on earth

Apatosaurus

This dinosaur had peg-like teeth for gathering leaves from plants. Apatosaurus was so big, it probably had to spend most of the day eating.

Mamenchisaurus

Mamenchisaurus had the longest neck of any animal ever – up to 15 metres. That's nearly three times as long as a giraffe's neck.

The long, thin tail was carried off the ground.

Lufengosaurus

This skeleton shows Lufengosaurus rearing up on its back legs.

Diplodocus

Diplodocus was the longest dinosaur of all – longer than a tennis court. Despite its massive size it only had a tiny brain.

Barosaurus had a strong, whip-like tail.

Plateosaurus

Plateosaurus was
always looking
for food to fill its
big, bulky body.

Barosaurus

Barosaurus was the
tallest of the
dinosaurs. It could
reach treetops as
high as a five-storey
building. Because of
its height, some
scientists think it
had eight hearts.

Saltasaurus

Saltasaurus' back and sides were
protected by bony plates and
lumps beneath its skin.

Can you
guess why
Saltasaurus
needed its
armour-plating?

Barosaurus'
heavy neck was
held up by strong,
ribbed bones.

Armoured tanks

Kentrosaurus

Kentrosaurus was a slow-moving plant-eater. It had bony plates and spines along its back. The pairs of spines above its back legs helped to protect it from attackers.

plates

spines

turtle-shaped head

belly armour

Minmi

Minmi was a small dinosaur that lived in Australia. It was so well protected that it had bony plates on its belly as well as its back.

Experts think that the bony plates along its neck and back helped Stegosaurus to keep cool in hot weather and warm in cold weather.

Stegosaurus

Stegosaurus was the largest of the plated dinosaurs. It ambled slowly along, munching on plants. Stegosaurus probably used its fierce spiked tail as a club to defend itself from hungry meat-eaters.

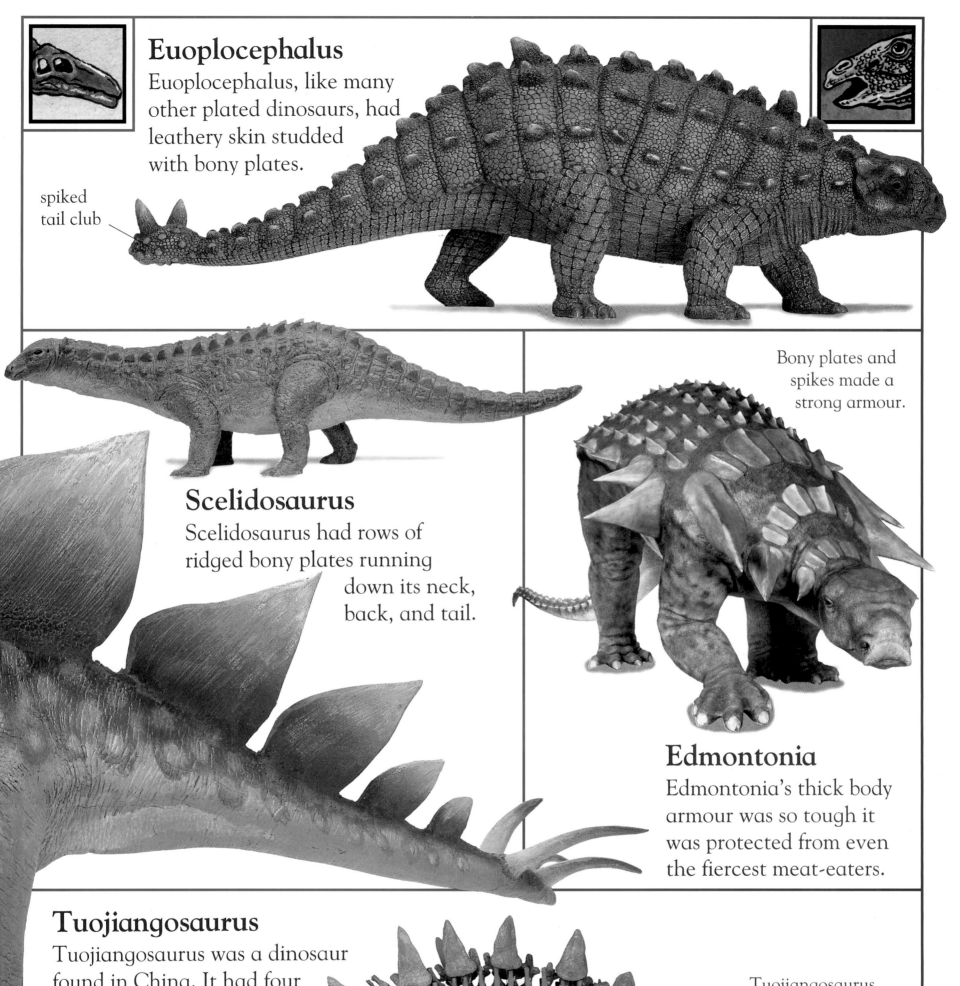

Euoplocephalus

Euoplocephalus, like many other plated dinosaurs, had leathery skin studded with bony plates.

spiked tail club

Bony plates and spikes made a strong armour.

Scelidosaurus

Scelidosaurus had rows of ridged bony plates running down its neck, back, and tail.

Edmontonia

Edmontonia's thick body armour was so tough it was protected from even the fiercest meat-eaters.

Tuojiangosaurus

Tuojiangosaurus was a dinosaur found in China. It had four sharp spikes on its tail. What do you think it used the spikes on its tail for?

Tuojiangosaurus kept its head close to the ground to find leaves to eat.

21

Leaf-eaters

Lesothosaurus

Lesothosaurus was a tiny dinosaur not much bigger than a dog. It looked a bit like a lizard standing up on its back legs.

Heterodontosaurus may have used its hands to dig in the sand for roots or to tear open insects' nests.

Heterodontosaurus

Heterodontosaurus was small and probably ate leaves and roots. It could run very fast to escape from hungry meat-eating dinosaurs.

three long toes on each foot

long toes with sharp claws

Hypsilophodon

Hypsilophodon was a very speedy dinosaur. It grazed in herds, which was much safer than roaming alone.

The front of Iguanodon's mouth was shaped like a beak.

Iguanodon

One of the best known dinosaurs, Iguanodon, was much bigger than many other leaf-eaters. It could probably walk on two legs, as well as on all fours.

Iguanodon had strange, spiked thumbs. It may have used them to defend itself.

Iguanodon's tail balanced its large body.

Hypsilophodon's long legs show that it was a fast runner.

Duckbilled dinosaurs

Saurolophus

Saurolophus had a flap of skin between its beak and crest. Scientists think the dinosaur used this to make loud, honking calls.

Edmontosaurus had powerful jaws and hundreds of teeth for chewing tough leaves.

Parasaurolophus' long crest was hollow inside.

Parasaurolophus

For a long time, experts thought Parasaurolophus' crest was used to help it breathe. Now they think it helped the dinosaur to make louder calls.

Edmontosaurus

Edmontosaurus wandered around in slow-moving herds. Like the other duckbilled dinosaurs, it ate plants.

Shantungosaurus

Shantungosaurus was probably the biggest duckbilled dinosaur.

bony,
hollow
crest

hatchet-
shaped
crest

Lambeosaurus

Lambeosaurus had a beak like a
duck's. It also had a hollow crest
shaped like a hatchet.

Corythosaurus

Corythosaurus means "helmet
lizard". It had a thin, flat
crest on its head. Scientists
think their crests helped
these dinosaurs to
recognize one
another.

The bony crest
formed part of
the skull.

Corythosaurus had
long fingers and
short claws.

Boneheads and horns

Styracosaurus
Styracosaurus was a horned-faced dinosaur. It had a head frill with sharp spikes.

Psittacosaurus
This early dinosaur was called Psittacosaurus, or "parrot reptile", because it had a beak like a parrot's.

Stegoceras
Stegoceras had a bony head shaped like an egg. Its stiff tail helped to balance the weight of its body.

Triceratops
Triceratops was like a huge rhinoceros with a massive, three-horned head. As it munched on plants it probably used its fierce-looking horns to defend itself against meat-eaters.

The tail was held rigid by lots of muscles and bones.

Can you think why Pachycephalosaurus needed a thick skull?

Pachycephalosaurus

This strange dinosaur had a bony head like a crash helmet. Experts think these dinosaurs had head-butting contests.

Chasmosaurus

Chasmosaurus had a huge head frill that stretched halfway down its back. It had a horn on its nose and two above its eyes. What do you think it used its horns for?

bony lump

neck frill

Pachyrhinosaurus

Pachyrhinosaurus' skull has a small horn in the middle of its neck frill.

Dinosaur nursery

Orodromeus

This model shows Orodromeus' babies hatching. Fossil eggs of this small, two-legged plant-eater have been found in North America.

Nesting together

Dinosaurs laid eggs, as do reptiles and birds. Scientists have found fossils of eggs, nests, and babies belonging to duckbilled dinosaurs called Maiasaura. Groups of female dinosaurs built their nests close together and looked after the babies once they had hatched.

The nests were mounds of earth hollowed out in the middle.

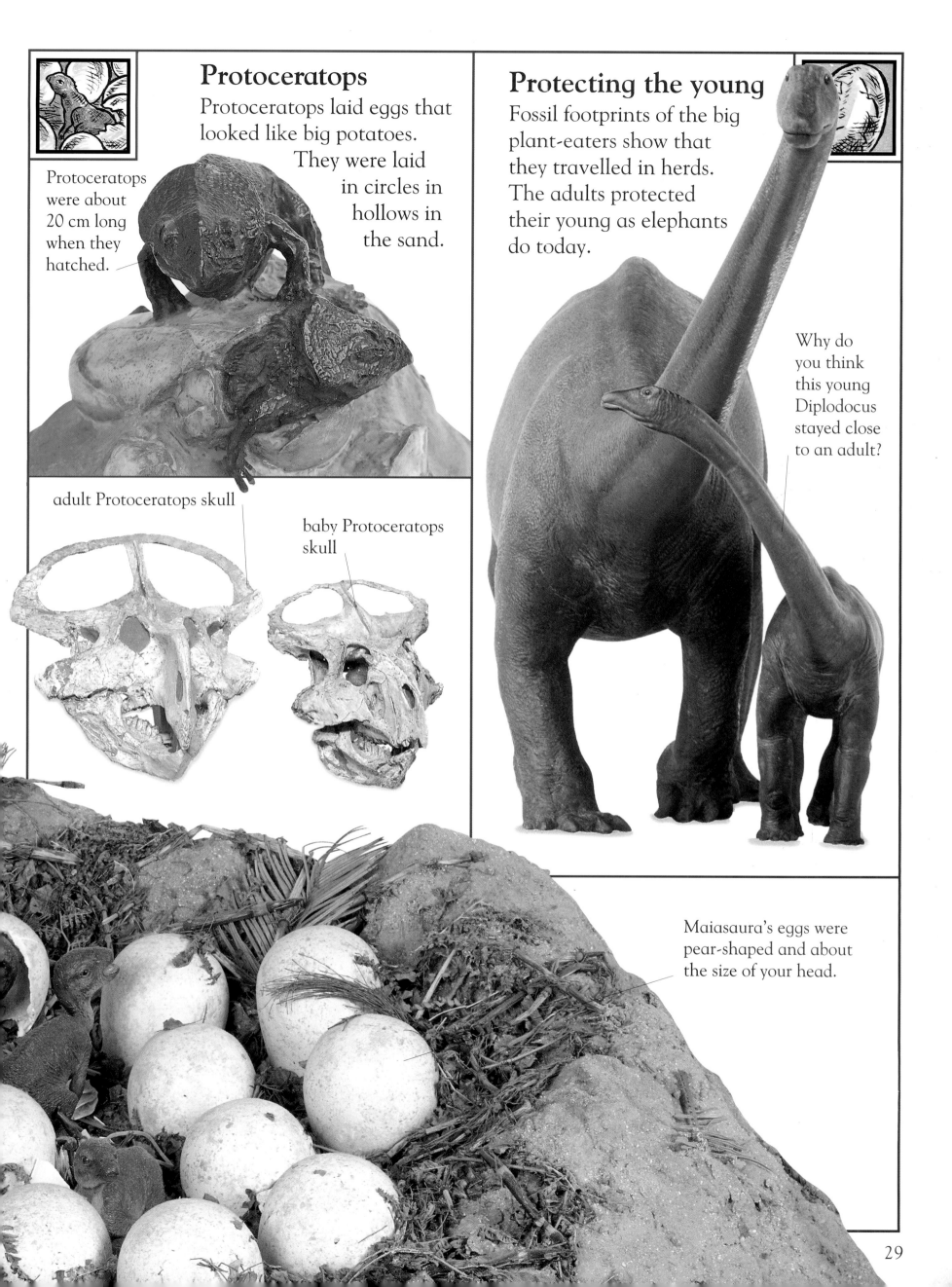

Protoceratops

Protoceratops laid eggs that looked like big potatoes. They were laid in circles in hollows in the sand.

Protoceratops were about 20 cm long when they hatched.

adult Protoceratops skull

baby Protoceratops skull

Protecting the young

Fossil footprints of the big plant-eaters show that they travelled in herds. The adults protected their young as elephants do today.

Why do you think this young Diplodocus stayed close to an adult?

Maiasaura's eggs were pear-shaped and about the size of your head.

29

In scale

From big to little

Many people think that all dinosaurs were huge, but in fact they came in all shapes and sizes, from the gigantic Barosaurus to the tiny Compsognathus.

Did you spot any of these dinosaurs earlier in the book?

Corythosaurus
10 metres long

Stegosaurus
9 metres long

Iguanodon
9 metres long

Hypsilophodon
2.3 metres long

Deinonychus
3 metres long

Pachycephalosaurus
4.6 metres long

Barosaurus
23–27 metres long

Tyrannosaurus
12 metres long

Euoplocephalus
7 metres long

Compsognathus
70 centimetres long

Triceratops
9 metres long

Gallimimus
6 metres long

Index